D1262947

IN MY BACKYARD

WITHDRAWN

moles

by Kate Riggs

CREATIVE EDUCATION • CREATIVE PAPERBACKS

Published by Creative Education and Creative Paperbacks
P.O. Box 227, Mankato, Minnesota 56002
Creative Education and Creative Paperbacks are imprints of
The Creative Company
www.thecreativecompany.us

Design and production by Chelsey Luther
Art direction by Rita Marshall
Printed in China

Photographs by Alamy (David Cole), Animals Animals (Habicht,
Michael), Corbis (Creativ Studio Heinemann/imageBROKER,
Solvin Zankl/Nature Picture Library), Dreamstime (Sergey
Galushko, Brian Grant, Pavel Gribkov, Isselee, Andrey
Pavlov, Alexander Potapov, Prillfoto, Sergio Schnitzler),
Flickr (audreyjm529), iStockphoto (Antagain, juefraphoto,
merobson1, Tramper2), Shutterstock (ajt, Eric Isselee, Madlen,
Serg64), SuperStock (David Cole/age fotostock)

Library of Congress Cataloging-in-Publication Data
Riggs, Kate.
Moles / by Kate Riggs.
p. cm. — (In my backyard)
Includes bibliographical references and index.
Summary: A high-interest introduction to the life cycle of
moles, including how pups develop, their varied diet, threats
from predators, and the underground habitats of these
backyard animals.

ISBN 978-1-60818-700-3 (hardcover)
ISBN 978-1-62832-296-5 (pbk)
ISBN 978-1-56660-736-0 (eBook)
1. Moles—Juvenile literature.

QL737.S76 R54 2016
599.33/5—dc23   2015039245

CCSS: RI.1.1, 2, 3, 4, 5, 6, 7; RI.2.1, 2, 4, 5, 6, 7, 10; RF.1.1, 3, 4;
RF.2.3, 4

First Edition HC 9 8 7 6 5 4 3 2 1
First Edition PBK 9 8 7 6 5 4 3 2 1

Contents

You are standing in your yard. The grass is very dry. It hasn't rained in a long time. Suddenly, you hear a sound. *Rip, rip, rip.* It is a mole tearing through dirt!

True moles are found only in North America and Europe.

In the spring, baby moles are born. Two to seven are born in each litter. Baby moles are called pups. Pups leave their mothers after one to two months.

Pups do not open their eyes until they are about three weeks old.

Moles belong to the talpid animal family. Their bodies are shaped for living in tunnels. Strong claws help moles dig. Their fur is thick and dark.

Moles have an extra thumb next to the regular one on their front paws.

Secretive moles stay underground. They can breathe, see, and hear down there. Have you ever seen a mole? Often, a molehill is the only sign it leaves!

Star-nosed moles have the best sense of touch, thanks to their unique nose.

Moles eat worms they find in the dirt. They store a lot of worms for the winter. They feed on nuts and insects, too. Sometimes a mole will eat small animals when it is aboveground.

A mole can eat more than 50 pounds (22.7 kg) of worms in a year.

Moles stay busy in their tunnels. They live alone. When a female makes a nest, you can see a big molehill. A line of smaller molehills means a deep tunnel is there.

Males dig long, straight tunnels, but females branch off in many directions.

Not many animals eat moles. Predators include some types of owls, snakes, and foxes. People are the biggest threat to moles.

To escape predators, a mole can run backward as fast as it can run forward.

People may not like having molehills in their yard. So they try to get rid of moles. Look around outside for small mounds of dirt. There may be a mole down there!

Dogs and other animals may smell moles underground and try to find them.

Activity: Be the Mole

A mole spends most of its life underground. Do you think it would get lonely? What would it see and smell? Imagine what things would be like from its point of view.

Materials you need: pencil or marker and paper

A Mole's Tale

1. Picture yourself as a mole living underground. Try writing a short story about what you would do, hear, taste, see, and smell every day. Go outside and do some research. Look at the grass and dirt around you. Write down what it looks, smells, and feels like. Be sure to add those details to your story!

2. Give your mole a name and a problem to solve. Maybe you hit something mysterious while digging a tunnel. Maybe some other animal has eaten all the worms, and you're running out of food. What happens next?

3. Is your mole a hero or a villain? Make up other characters for the mole to talk to.

Read your story to a friend. Maybe she will want to draw pictures to go along with it!

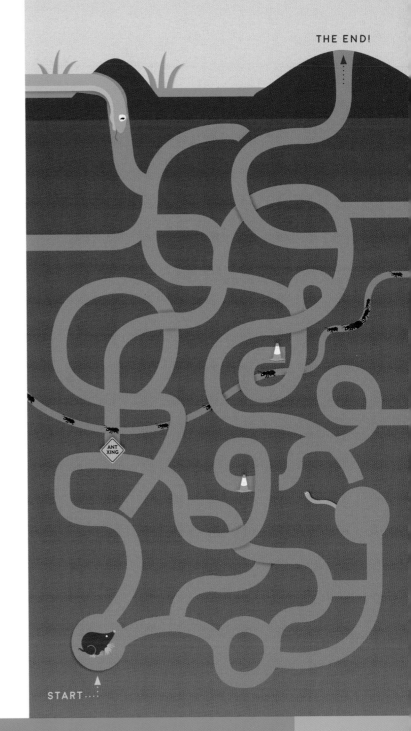

THE END!

ANT XING

START

 Glossary

litter: a group of animal babies born at the same time

molehill: a small pile of dirt that sticks up from an underground mole tunnel

predators: animals that hunt other animals for food

talpid: a member of the animal family that includes moles, shrew moles, and desmans

Read More

Owings, Lisa. *Star-Nosed Mole*.
Minneapolis: Bellwether Media, 2014.

Sebastian, Emily. *Moles*.
New York: PowerKids Press, 2012.

Websites

Activity Village: Mole Activities
http://www.activityvillage.co.uk/moles
Make a mole puppet and print out pages to color and
write on.

Easy Science for Kids: Moles
http://easyscienceforkids.com/all-about-moles/
Learn more about moles and watch a video about star-
nosed moles.

Note: Every effort has been made to ensure that the websites listed above are suitable for
children, that they have educational value, and that they contain no inappropriate mate-
rial. However, because of the nature of the Internet, it is impossible to guarantee that these
sites will remain active indefinitely or that their contents will not be altered.

Index